The Human Person, African Ubuntu And The Dialogue Of Civilisations

Published by
Adonis & Abbey Publishers Ltd
P.O. Box 43418
London
SE11 4XZ
http://www.adonis-abbey.com
Email: editor@adonis-abbey.com

First Edition, February 2009

Copyright © Chris Vervliet

British Library Cataloguing-in-Publication Data
A catalogue record for this book is available from the British
Library

ISBN 9781906704-28-5 (PB)

The moral right of the author has been asserted

The Human Person, African Ubuntu And The Dialogue Of Civilisations

By

Chris Vervliet

iv

Table of Contents

vi

PREFACE

History today is at a watershed.

Looming in front of us is the menace of a clash of civilisations, as predicted by the American academic Samuel Huntington. Luring our hopes is the perspective of an ultimate convergence of civilisations, as predicted by a variety of authors ranging from Léopold Senghor to Francis Fukuyama[1].

This is what this book is all about. In an age when much is being said about the clash of civilisations, we have discovered concerns that transcend the boundaries of civilisations and answers that are remarkable through their similarity. This book explores these remarkable similarities.

In the first chapter of this book, we return to the first decades of post-colonial Africa. We rediscover the ideas of men such as Leopold Sédar Senghor, Julius Nyerere and Kwame Nkrumah. We also pause at some of their critics.

From there on, we move on to present-day Africa. We focus on Ubuntu, a human-person centred philosophy of contemporary South Africa. We do not limit ourselves to an abstract philosophical description but also point at the

---

[1]Samuel Huntington and Francis Fukuyama were the proponents of a major intellectual controversy in the nineties. According to Huntington, the end of the Cold War would rejuvenate age-old conflicts between civilisations, that had been temporarily suppressed by the Cold War. To the contrary, Francis Fukuyama predicted a convergence of civilisations towards a free-market system and parliamentary democracy. Léopold Senghor, former president of Senegal, introduced the notion of the Civilization of the Universal, to be achieved through the cross-fertilisation of cultures.

vii

attempts to implement the principles in practice. In doing so, we note some remarkable differences with the communal thinking of the sixties and seventies.

The second chapter widens the thinking on the human person and the community by introducing European and American personalism as well as the Moroccan author Lahbabi's view on "*Shakçânyya*" (or "Muslim personalism", as he calls it).

The final chapter compares Ubuntu, Christian-democratic personalism and *Shakçânyya* and reflects on their differences and similarities.

It has become fashionable in political science to disregard ideology. This is a regrettable mistake. Decision-makers carry with them the burden of their convictions and perceptions. I am not so naive to believe that the exchange of ideas may by itself suffice to bring about the harmony of civilizations. Nevertheless, I hope that the awareness that across eras, continents and civilisations, common questions are being asked, common concerns invoked and similar answers suggested, may at least facilitate the mutual dialogue.

Chris Vervliet

CHAPTER 1

FROM AFRICAN COMMUNAL THINKERS TO TODAY'S UBUNTU

Much of the thinking on clashes or convergence of civilisations is written from a first world background. To avoid this bias, we deliberately start our analysis in Africa. We explore the writings of African leaders and thinkers of the sixties and seventies, such as Leopold Sedar Senghor, Julius Nyerere, Kwame Nkrumah - among others. This was an age in which the post-colonial leaders sought to reaffirm African dignity and African authenticity – by pointing at the communal nature of African society. From there on we move beyond the disillusionment, to today's Ubuntu thinking, prevailing in today's South Africa.

1.1 Leopold Senghor (1906-2001)

Leopold Senghor was president of Senegal from 1960 till 1980. With the Martinique author Aimé Césaire (1913 - 2008), he was one of the leading thinkers behind the *Négritude* movement, which sought to promote negro-African cultural authenticity. For Senghor, the authenticity of Africans was their communal way of living. Although he used the word "socialism", he hastened to say that African socialism differed from European socialism in that it was not based on class struggle or class contradictions, but on brotherhood, community life and mutual love.

9

> "Although all the present political regimes -democracy, socialism, Communism- have as their goal totalization and socialization without depersonalization, they fail in their attempt. This is because they sacrifice the part to the whole, the person to the collectivity. (...) Because the Negro Africans have kept a sense of brotherhood and dialogue, because they are inspired by religions that preach love and, above all, because they live those religions, they can propose positive solutions for the construction of the international as well as the national community. The importance of love as essential energy, the stuff of life, is at the heart of Négritude, underlying the black man's ontology."
> (Senghor, 1964: 148).

At some occasions, the Senegalese president used the notion "African socialism". At others, he used the word "communalism".

Despite his passion for *Négritude,* Senghor admired French culture and was a member of the prestigious *Académie Française.* By interfecundating one another, cultures all over the world can contribute to the construction of the "Civilization of the Universal". However, in order to be able to contribute to the construction of this Civilization of the Universal, all nations had to be conscious of what they had to offer to the world. Hence, the need for *Négritude* as an ingredient in the wider construction of the Civilization of the Universal.

> "It is a question of placing our nation not only in the Africa of today, but also in the Civilization of the Universal yet to be built. The latter, as I like to repeat, will be a symbiosis of the most fecundating elements of all civilizations." (Senghor, 1964: 83).

10

In developing this reasoning, Senghor was strongly influenced by the French Jesuit palaeontologist Teilhard de Chardin. The latter tried to reconcile the scientific evidence for evolution theory with his religious belief. In doing so, he came up with a theory of 'becoming', that started with inanimate matter (atoms), which gradually evolved toward more complex aggregates.

"Thus, from the nucleus of the atom to the living being, we progress toward a greater complexity, as we pass through the atom, the molecule, and the cell." (Senghor, referring to Teilhard de Chardin, 1964: 135).

Beyond a critical threshold of complexity, consciousness and reflection appeared. Reflection developed into co-reflection (reflecting with one another) and hence socialization. Eventually, civilizations appeared. The ultimate stage, Teilhard believed, was the progress toward God (the point Omega) - to be achieved through the interfecundating of civilizations.

Quoting Teilhard de Chardin, Senghor writes:

"Teilhard restores our dignity and invites us to the dialogue. He (=Teilhard) writes: 'Before the last upheavals that awakened the earth, peoples were only superficially alive; a world of energies was still asleep within each of them. Well, I imagine that these powers, still dormant within each natural human unity, in Europe, Asia, everywhere, are stirring and trying to come to light at this very moment; not to oppose and devour one another, but to rejoin and interfecundate one another. Fully conscious nations are needed for a total earth.'
This is the justification for our nationalism and our Négritude. " (Senghor, 1964: 140).

11

1.2 Julius Nyerere (1922 – 1999)

Julius Nyerere was the spiritual father of a philosophy and policy, which became known as "Ujamaa". In 1961, he led the former British protectorate of Tanganyika to independence. Some years later he became president of Tanzania, which was formed by the joining of Tanganyika and the island of Zanzibar. In 1965, the newly formed Republic of Tanzania was transformed into a one-party system. According to Nyerere, this move was needed for stability.

In 1967, Nyerere outlined his major policy principles in a declaration, which became known as the Arusha declaration. Self-reliance of developing countries and the creation of a socialist society were central concerns. However, Nyerere hastened to point out how his African socialism differed from European socialism.

The reasoning displays similarities with Senghor's.

> "European socialism was born of the Agrarian Revolution and the Industrial Revolution which followed it. The former created the 'land' and the 'landless' classes in society; the latter produced the modern capitalist and the industrial proletariat.
>
> These two revolutions planted the seeds of conflict within society, and not only was European socialism born of that conflict, but its apostles sanctified the conflict itself into a philosophy. (...)
>
> The foundation, and the objective, of African socialism is the extended family. (....). '
>
> 'Ujamaa', then, or 'familyhood' describes our socialism.

12

It is opposed to capitalism, which seeks to build a
happy society on the basis of the exploitation of man by
man; and it is equally opposed to doctrinaire socialism
which seeks to build its happy society on a philosophy
of inevitable conflict between man and man." (Nyerere)

Tanzania was one of the few African countries not to
adopt the former colonial language (English) as national
language after independence.   Instead, it opted for
Swahili, as a testimony of the dedication towards African
authenticity. Ujamaa itself is a Swahili word with an Arab
root[2]. Translations into English range from 'familyhood'
to 'brotherhood'. Pivotal in the implementation of Ujamaa
was the creation of communal villages in which the land
was   collectively   held   and   production   collectively
organized (so-called ujamaa villages).

Initially, the rural population lived in dispersed
family smallholdings. Resettling the rural population into
villages of sufficient sizes, so it was hoped, would
facilitate the access to social infrastructure (schools,
clinics...) and increase agricultural production. Initially,
merely 5% of rural population lived in villages. By the
mid-seventies, about 60% of rural population had been
resettled into Ujamaa villages.

In the late sixties and early seventies, the Ujamaa
policy was often hailed by intellectuals and academics as
an example of how economic development could be
matched with an egalitarian society. Not surprisingly,
Tanzania was one of the major recipients of development
assistance. However, by the mid-seventies it became
apparent that Ujamaa did not live up to its promises.

---

[2]Jama is an Arab word, referring to a collectivity of people.
Depending on the context, it can be translated as 'group', 'party'
or 'congregation'.

13

From 1975 onwards, the Tanzanian government began to reverse its economic policy. Nyerere himself retired as president in 1985. Although his policies have largely been abandoned, he has remained a symbol of post-colonial Africa.

1.3 Kwame Nkrumah (1909 – 1972)

As president of the first African colony to gain independence (Ghana), Kwame Nkrumah was the foremost proponent of Pan-Africanism. Born in 1909 he initially embarked upon a career in teaching. In 1935 he went studying in the United States and combined his studies with a part-time lectureship in Negro history. In 1945 he went to London to complete his doctorate, where he met the leading Panafricanist author George Padmore. During his time in London, he became the leader of a secret organisation 'The Circle", dedicated to the unity and independence of West Africa. In 1947 he wrote his first book, Towards Colonial Freedom. That same year he returned to Ghana (or the Gold Coast as it was named at the time). In the ensuing years, periods of political action and detention followed one another, culminating in an electoral victory in the 1956 pre-independence elections and Ghana's declaration of independence in 1958. As head of the newly independent state, he tried to rally other African colonies around the cause of independence.

After establishing a one-party state with himself as Life President in 1964, he was eventually overthrown in a military coup in 1966, while on a state visit to North Vietnam. He died in exile in 1972.

Just like Senghor cherished Négritude and Nyerere promoted Ujamaa, Nkrumah established his own

14

doctrine, *Consciencism*, which initially displayed similarities with both Négritude and Ujamaa.

As far back as 1949, Nkrumah had proclaimed his commitment to socialism. The 1949 draft of the program of his Convention People's Party, stated (art. 8) that the party aimed at founding "a Socialist State in which all men and women (would) have equal opportunity and where there would be no capitalist exploitation." This draft was adopted two years later.

The first edition of his book, Consciencism (1964), reflected the view that in pre-colonial Africa, exploitation of man by man and class struggle were unknown. In doing so, he linked his commitment to socialism with African traditions and pre-empted the objection that he was importing a foreign ideology (Houtondji, 1983: 146).

Over time, however, one notices a gradual shift in his thinking. A pamphlet entitled "Two Myths" (1968), testifies of the evolution in the thinking of Nkrumah.

"Today, the phrase 'African socialism' seems to espouse the view that the traditional African society was a classless society imbued with the spirit of humanism and to express a nostalgia for that spirit. Such a conception of socialism makes a fetish of the communal African society. But an idyllic, African classless society (in which there were no rich and no poor) enjoying a drugged serenity is certainly a facile simplification; there is no historical or even anthropological evidence for any such society. I am afraid the realities of African society were somewhat more sordid."

This change of heart is no coincidence. By that time, the political context had changed completely. Some years before, he had been overthrown by a military coup and was as a result living in exile in North Vietnam.

15

1.4 Child in time

Is there such a thing like authentic cultural identity or are cultures too diverse and too loose to be "grasped"? Cultural identity is often spoken about yet difficult to grasp. The concept of Négritude rested on three assumptions:

(i) that cultural identity is not a fictional concept, but does exist;
(ii) that Negro-Africans share some common cultural traits;
(iii) that the essence of negro-African culture is situated in the communal way of living.

These views were not confined to the world of politics. The fifties and sixties witnessed a multitude of publications, which attempted to define "African identity"[3].

An author who deserves particular attention is John Mbiti (°1931), theologian, author, teacher and pastor. Born in Kenya between the two World Wars, John Mbiti zoomed in on the relationship between the Gospel, local culture and traditional religion. According to Mbiti, Africans are by their nature, spiritual. Just like other writers of his generation, Mbiti also pointed at the communal nature of African society. While Descartes stated, *"I think, therefore I am"*, the African, according to Mbiti, stated: *"I am, because you are, you are because I am"* (Mbiti, 1969: 109).

Ideas and convictions seldom originate in a vacuum.

---

[3]See for instance Placide Tempels, La Philosophy Bantoue (1949). Also see the German author Janheinz Jahn (1918-1973).

They reflect the spirit and the concerns of their time and place.

The nineteenth century reflected the influence of Enlightenment thinking and rationalism. With faith in progress also came the belief in superior (more advanced) societies and primitive societies (those that were lagging behind). This conviction underlined British imperialist thinking and provided a legitimation for colonialism.

Disillusionment with the age of mechanisation and industrialisation resulted in a gradual reappraisal of so-called 'primitive' societies. The First World War shattered whatever was left of the faith in progress.

The nineteen twenties and thirties saw the rise of the functionalist school in anthropology. According to functionalism, rituals and customs, which, judged by European culture seemed meaningless, served a specific purpose within their own cultural context. Judged by the standards of European culture, "primitive" rituals and customs seemed meaningless. However, within their own cultural context, they made up a consistent and logical whole.

Malinowksi, one of the leading functionalist anthropologists, wrote in 1930:

> " Many of us ... see a menace to all real spiritual and artistic values in the aimless advance of modern mechanization. One of the refuges from this mechanical prison of culture is the study of primitive forms of human life as they still exist in remote parts of our globe. Anthropology, to me at least, as a romantic escape from our over standardized culture." (quoted in Houtondji, 1983: 157).

Senghor and Césaire were familiar with functionalist thinking. It undoubtedly influenced their concept of

17

Négritude as a consistent cultural system.

Two other elements also played a role. The fifties and the sixties were the age of decolonization. The decolonization was not only a political movement but also an emancipatory movement, which sought to affirm the dignity of the formerly colonized peoples. Négritude, Ujamaa and Consciencism all fit in with this endeavour.

A second element was the Cold War. In the sixties, the cold war was at its peak. The African authors whom we have quoted did not want to align themselves with either one of the opposing blocs and instead opted for non-alignment. Capitalism was perceived negatively because of its connotations with the former colonial system and with exploitation. Socialism, Soviet style, was considered too materialistic and too conflictual. Hence the promotion of an African-styled socialism – less conflictual and more spiritual.

From a practical point of view, many a third world intellectual perceived centrally planned economies as the best way to development. From today's point of view, this may seem strange. Today, our perspective on the inefficiency of centrally planned economies is marked by the collapse of the Soviet Union and its Eastern European allies. Four decades ago, the perspective was totally different. The Soviet Union was winning the space race-having launched the first satellite and the first man into space. Not surprisingly, the intellectual communalist thinking went hand in hand with economic policies in which central planning and parastatals were accorded a leading role.

18

1.5 Critics

All this seems to suggest that the communalist thinking of the sixties rested on a wide consensus. This was not so.

We already pointed at the shift in the thinking of Kwame Nkrumah. Something similar could be observed when Mozambique and Angola gained independence in the early seventies. The liberation movements that came to power had had close contacts with the banned Portuguese communist party. For them, what mattered was "scientific socialism", not a "retrograde" belief in traditional communal values.

A fundamental critique has been raised by Paulin Houtondji.

> "(when we use the phrase traditional African civilization), we ignore or pretend to ignore, the fact that African traditions are no more homogenous than those of any other continent, that cultural traditions are always a complex heritage, contradictory and heterogeneous, an open set of options (...). We ignore, or pretend to ignore the fact that cultural traditions can remain alive only if they are exploited anew (...). Above all, we ignore or pretend to ignore the fact that African cultural traditions are not closed, that they did not stop when colonization started but embrace colonial and post-colonial cultural life." (Hountondji, 1983: 162).

As time proceeded, came the hindsight of history.

In the age of the Cold War, the ideological debate centred on who owned the means of production. The end of the Cold War muted the relevance of this ideological debate. Moreover, while in the sixties, central planning was looked upon by many developing countries as the most effective way to development, the economic collapse of the Soviet Union and the Eastern European Countries rendered this idea obsolete.

Secondly, by the nineties, it had become apparent that the first decades of African independence had not delivered the promises once hoped for.

The Ubuntu philosophy occupies a prominent status in the social and political thinking of present-day South Africa. It shares two characteristics with earlier communal thinking. Just like the communalist thinking of the sixties, Ubuntu is rooted in a search toward African dignity. We Africans have something to offer to the world, is the fundamental message across the decades. Just like the communalist thinking of the sixties, Ubuntu finds the answer in harmony of the individual (the person) and the community. *"Umuntu ngumuntu ngabantu"*, a person is a person through other persons.

However, at the same time, it tries to get to grips with the hindsight of history. For example: the focus is not longer on the ownership of the means of production, but rather on – for instance- how to introduce an Ubuntu-inspired management-style in corporate life or on the implications of Ubuntu for welfare politics.

Also, a very specific contextual aspect needs to be mentioned. Most literature on Ubuntu appeared in the nineties, i.e. in the aftermath of the dismantling of apartheid. This also explains some of the themes being discussed. Desmond Tutu for instance contrasts Ubuntu with racism but at the same time relates it with forgiveness.

In the following paragraphs, we will try to give an overview of the principal elements of the Ubuntu-philosophy.

1.6 The human person: community-bound

The philosophy of Ubuntu is reflected in the proverb:

> *"Umuntu ngumuntu ngabantu"*, where:
> *umuntu*[4] (noun), is the singular for "human being, person";
> *ngumuntu* (verb), means "is a person, becomes a person"
> *"nga"* is a prefix meaning, "through, by means of",
> *"abantu"*, is the plural of "umuntu", thus meaning "persons".

Ubuntu itself means humanity, human nature. "Uluntu", the Xhosa-word for "community", and "umuntu" (person)are related to the same root. The complementarity of umuntu ("the person") and "uluntu" (the community) is said to be inherent to African society, as is demonstrated by the fact that both words are derived from the same root.

As such, Ubuntu is part of an encompassing movement of reappraisal of the African 'heritage', which has grown throughout the nineties.

According to the Ubuntu philosophy, human beings achieve their fullness in the community. Several authors, writing from different perspectives, have this as common thread.

Dr. Ntate Koka (1927-2005), linked Ubuntu to Africa-centred education, which he called "Afrikalogy". "Afrikalogy" is a concept introduced by himself and stands for the systematic study of African concepts, precepts and culture – in order to develop an Africa-

---

[4]The word "umuntu" is Zulu. In Xhosa, the same concept is "umntu". Xhosa and Zulu both belong to the Nguni language group.

centred consciousness and rediscover the dignity of Africans (one notices here a similarity with Négritude).

> "As a Pan African African first you are to build on this state of "humaneness". There can be no peace in Africa until our humaneness is realised. Unless I realise that my beingness hangs on the beingness of the other. This is one aspect. I am because you are, and you are because I am. In the Rasta[5] world it is the I and I; that is a very deep philosophy; the I and I. That is I recognise the beingness of the other. I exist as the other exists." (interview with Ntate Koka, by N. Hlongwane and Q. Gabela).

Ntate Koka was involved with the South Africa Black Consciousness Movement in the seventies but later spend about two decades in exile.

Former Anglican archbishop and Nobel Peace Prize laureate Desmond Tutu relates the Ubuntu philosophy to his Christian beliefs. In the face of God, we are all children of one and the same heavenly father – made after the image of God. This means that people should respect one another and -projected onto the South African context- reject racism but at the same time be able to forgive.

Augustine Shutte, writing from a Catholic perspective, points at the similarities between the European Thomist tradition and the Ubuntu philosophy.

Thomism is named after Thomas of Aquino and has its origin in the medieval European Catholic tradition. In terms of the Thomism, man is a spiritual being, created in the image of God. The Universe reflects the harmony of

---

[5]Rasta is a reference to Ethiopia, which in Panafricanism is hailed as the oldest African state.

the Creation and is centred on man. Thomism has profound ethical implications, for instance with regard to the notion of "equitibility" and "fairness" in economic life. Today, the scientific claims of Thomism have been abandoned yet the ethical implications and the concept of Man as a spiritual being live on in Neo-Thomism.

The notion of Man as a spiritual being also pervades the Ubuntu philosophy. At the same time, Man as a spiritual being does not stand alone as an isolated individual, but is integrated into a wider whole.

The importance of burials and the evocation of ancestral spirits is often invoked as an illustration of this point[6]. In traditional African societies, there seems to be an inextricable bond between man, ancestors and whatever is regarded as the Supreme being. The departed remain part of the community. The community transcends the border of life and death.

> "An often ignored reason behind the easy acceptance of Christianity as a way of life on African soil lies in the fact that its message was first heard as a confirmation of the values and principles of Botho-Ubuntu taught, aspired to and striven for in the traditional African world-view". (Setiloane, 1988).

1.7 Ubuntu and economic life

Several authors and management consultants have tried to introduce the Ubuntu philosophy into corporate thinking. Reuel Khoza, former chairman of the South African electricity provider Eskom, points at the need to enrich corporate culture with African values and leadership style. Under his auspices, Eric Mafuna of

---

[6]See for example Louw, D.

consultancy Africa Now researched whether there was such a thing like an African leadership style, and if so, what it was all about.

A first characteristic, according to the findings, was the African ability to solve the paradoxes inherent to conflicts. The emphasis in African traditional societies on collective rather than individual rights and responsibilities, and the way disputes are dealt with, put the principle of fairness and the need to hear both sides at the centre of any problem.

In the corporate context, Ubuntu stands for a less hierarchical, more interactive management culture. Also, Ubuntu stands for a corporate environment where teamwork prevails over individualistic achievements and leadership is opened for consultation and reaches for sufficient consensus.

> "The most effective leader of all is one that is democratic, who has a knack for listening but who, at the end, is able to give bold leadership and make hard-nosed decisions." (R. Khoza, quoted in the Financial Mail).

By relating Ubuntu to corporate culture, Khoza adds a new perspective to the communal thinking of the sixties. The leaders of the latter days focused on who owned the means of production and invariably concluded that state ownership would be the best way to promote economic growth. Khoza, to the contrary, points at the need of entrepreneurship and thriving enterprises for the future of Africa.

Reuel Khoza is not alone. Lovemore Mbigi, professor and consultant, relates Ubuntu to corporate values such as accountability, bottom-up communication and empower-

24

ment, training, capacity building at grass-roots level, and continuous improvement teams.

"This emerging shop-floor democracy will empower the worker to contribute to wealth creation and to derive job satisfaction." (Mbigi, 2000).

Apart from that, Mbigi argues, it is required to pay attention to the emotional and spiritual values of an organization.

"But modern management thinking, practices, and literature are weak in managing emotional and spiritual resources, which also help determine the value of an organization." (Mbigi, 2000).

As an alternative, he suggests to introduce African spirit religion into corporate thinking.

"In African spirit religion, the spirit represents our ultimate real self, our inner self and total being, and our total consciousness. The spirit is who we really are. In terms of management, spirit is the ultimate energy and consciousness of an organization." (Mbigi, 2000).

In this respect, he draws on the metaphor of the "African spirit model". This model serves as a tool to capture the prevailing corporate culture and start the transformation toward new corporate values. His model introduces some archetypes of African spirits. "Shave" ("sha" is Zulu for "new"), for example, is the spirit of the outsider who comes to the organization, usually as a "Knight in Shining Armor" to solve all problems. This spirit is innovative and creative. Ability and creativity are among his principal qualities. Rarely are "Shave" people accepted in

25

organizations. Usually they are just tolerated. However, it is good thing for organizations to attract the maverick from outside to help with innovation – as they question established ways of working. A totally different character is the "Sangoma" (the divination spirit). The Sangoma possesses authority, he incorporates the claim on knowing the truth. Experts and specialists in an organization have this spirit. This spirit can be traditionalist and reduce the rate of learning in an organization and therefore, its capacity to change. Teams need to have Shave and Sangoma.

Through workshops and group discussions, people are encouraged to determine which "spirits" correspond to the actual state of their organization. From the actual state of affairs, one can then move on to a program of change.

So far, we focused on the impact of Ubuntu on corporate thinking.

At the same time, Ubuntu is associated with social welfare policy. The White Paper on Social Welfare of the South African Government (1997) explicitly refers to Ubuntu.

> "The principle of caring for each other's well-being will be promoted, and a spirit of mutual support fostered.
> Each individual's humanity is ideally expressed through his or her relationship with others and theirs in turn through recognition of the individual's humanity. Ubuntu means that people are people through other people. It also acknowledges both the rights and the responsibilities of every citizen in promoting individual and societal well-being."

1.8 Ubuntu: involvement through participation

Ubuntu refers to the complementarity of the individual and the community. Directly linked to this, is the idea of participating in community life. This community involvement is reflected, for instance, in self-help organisations and in the notion of interactive democracy.

The Masakhane campaign, which the South African government launched in the mid nineties, was a case in point of the former. Masakhane means *"let us build one another up"*. The Masakhane campaign was launched simultaneously with the Reconstruction and Development Program, the goal of which was to extend social services to the whole South African population. The objective of the Masakhane programme was to encourage the payment of residential services, rent and mortgages in black communities, which had a history of non-payment as a political protest. It did so by appealing to the responsibility of the community.

Another example frequently cited as an example of communal self-help are the so-called "stokvels", informal saving schemes, in which a group of friends, neighbours, members of a same family, of a same church... agree to contribute a fixed amount of money to a common pool at regular intervals. The money is raised either by fee contribution or at parties, which the members organise for one another. In the latter case, the "profit" of the evening goes to the savings scheme. Membership of a stokvel is voluntarily and mutual trust is pivotal. The money pooled can be used for special occasions, such as to pay for a burial or to help a member who wants to buy a house or start a business.

Ubuntu is also frequently cited in relation to

consensus building and participation of the community in decision-making. In this respect, Ubuntu is sometimes contrasted with the majority rule underlying Western democracy. Occasionally, multi-party systems are blamed for undermining the principle of solidarity in traditional African political culture. However, most of the time, Ubuntu is invoked to refer to the capacity of traditional African culture to pursue consensus and reconciliation. In traditional African tribal decision-making, it is claimed, every one had an equal chance to voice his opinion. Through lengthy discussions and concession ("indaba"), consensus was eventually reached. In this respect, Ubuntu refers to a consensual democracy where participation is pivotal, and where, through participation and concession, group solidarity is enforced.

However, some tricky questions remain with regard to this consensual democracy: how to balance consensus and group solidarity with the safeguard of minority views. Some authors argue that the respect for minority views is inherent to the process of participation and concession. Others, however, argue that this notion of group consensus and group solidarity has something inherently overwhelming and as such will easily deviate into an oppressive conformity and loyalty to the group (see for a discussion Dirk Louw, 2002).

1.9 Critics

Although the Ubuntu philosophy has achieved a prominent status in the social and political thinking of present-day South Africa, it is not without critics.

The first critique boils down to the question: was traditional African society really as idyllic as Ubuntu wants us to believe? Ubuntu is said to romanticize the African past, in much the same way as *Négritude* in the sixties did. UNISA-professor Tinyiko Sam Maluleke comments:

> "Such romanticism, however, is ultimately negative towards African culture. For it must be pointed out that African culture could not have remained thus indefinitely, and things have 'moved on' in African culture so that a 'return' is not only impossible but perhaps also undesirable. However, the Négritude school of thought remains popular and is restated in a variety of ways even in our own times. (...) Today we see a resurgence of 'negritude' in the popularity of the concept Ubuntu'

Maluleke calls on African intellectuals to reconnect to African culture, yet cautions:

> "My call for African intellectuals to reconnect to African culture is not a call for the resuscitation of romantic negritude. (...) It is rather a call to a mature re-appropriation of past and present manifestations of African culture within, because of and in spite of oppressive and racist conditions."

A second critique raises a totally different question. Even if traditional African societies were as communal as Ubuntu and Négritude claim, is that what we really want?

Themba Sono, professor and politician, discusses the issue from the perspective of an African intellectual's desire for open thinking. The role of the group, according to Sono, can be

> "overwhelming, totalistic, even totalitarian. Group psychology, though parochially and narrowly based (...) nonetheless pretends universality (...). Discursive

rationality is overwhelmed by emotional identity, by the obsession to identify with and by the longing to conform to. To agree is more important than to disagree, conformity is cherished more than innovation. Tradition is venerated, continuity revered, change feared and difference shunned. Heresies (i.e. the innovative creations of intellectual African individuals or refusals to participate in communalism) are not tolerated in such communities." (Sono, 1994: 7).

2.0 Summary

In this chapter, we explored the diverse facets of Ubuntu and compared it to the African communal thinking of the sixties and seventies. Glancing back at the chapter, one can distil a triple concern in the Ubuntu philosophy.

First of all, a concern for African self-esteem, as reflected in the effort to link Ubuntu to traditional communal living. Secondly, a concern to overcome the duality of 'individual' and 'community' by pointing at the complementarity of both. People grow as human beings in interaction with the community of which they are part. Thirdly, a concern to attribute to human beings a spiritual dimension, be it in a Christian perspective or in a less specific religious perspective.

All this is done in a context, which is different from the sixties and the seventies. As such, the debate does not longer centre on the ownership of the means of production, but rather on how to implement Ubuntu into management practices or how to infuse more participation into the formal democracy.

We also some noted some of the questions and objections surrounding Ubuntu. Did the idyllic African communal society ever exist or is part of a romanticized past? And even if it did, how can one guard against it becoming too overwhelming?

CHAPTER 2

PERSONALISM, CHRISTIAN-DEMOCRACY AND SHAKçÂNYYA

From Africa, we now expand the debate. In the nineteenth century, the scientific and industrial revolutions challenged the traditional views on what being human meant. Later, the upheavals of the early twentieth century – First World War, economic crisis, rise of totalitarian ideologies- provoked an intense philosophical debate on the essence of human dignity and on the relation between the individual and the community.

In this context personalism arose. In the personalist tradition, human beings are endowed with an inalienable human dignity. Human beings attain their dignity by being part of the community – although the personalist tradition is swift to add that they retain a proper identity and should not be reduced to the collectivity. This is reflected in the choice of the word "person" to reflect what being human is all about.

2.1 The philosophical prelude

The Middle Ages were pervaded by a worldview in which man, considered to be God's creation, was at the centre of the universe. The universe itself reflected divine harmony. Inherent in this worldview, known as Thomism, was a belief of social harmony. Society had to reflect fairness and equitibility.

From the sixteenth century onwards, the scientific revolution intruded into the certainties of the Thomist worldview. Sir Isaac Newton discovered the law of gravity, which explained why the earth orbited the sun – not vice versa. As the centuries progressed, man became more and more removed from the centre of the universe; a seemingly meaningless piece of dust in a universe that at every new discovery turned out to be larger than imagined ever before.

By the mid-nineteenth century Darwin demonstrated that all species were subjected to the principle of evolution. Man, who five centuries before was at the centre of the universe, turned out to be related to the ape.

The German philosopher Rudolph Hermann Lotze (1817 - 1881) tried to come to grips with these discoveries. Lotze lectured in medicine and philosophy and tried to reconcile the world of scientific laws with ethical and religious ideals. According to Lotze, nature is governed by mechanical law, to which the human body too, is subjected. However, the mechanical laws of the universe fail to explain sensations, perceptions, forms of thinking, ethical and religious feelings. They leave no room for human purposes and ideals and as such are inadequate for the explanation of life. There must be something else, which Lotze called the soul.

Through this reasoning, Lotze tried to maintain the notion of man as a somehow special being in a world that was gradually becoming disenchanted. His notion of man influenced the later personalist thinkers, in particular Borden Parker Bowne (1847-1910) who was the founder of the American personalist school. He had studied in Germany and had met there Rudolph Hermann Lotze. In 1908, while teaching at Boston University, he published his major work "Personalism"

The key to reality, according to Bowne, is the thinking self that interacts with other selves in a world where ethical achievement is the primary goal. Identity is the

34

key to personality. Society consists of "interacting persons", dependent on the "Supreme Person, God". Although the thinking of Bowne was not politically motivated, it paid much attention to the notion of freedom. Knowledge requires an effort of searching the truth. This requires freedom of thought.

Through Borden Barker Bowne, Boston University was for decades to come the centre of the American school of Personalism. A Californian school of Personalism was later established by Ralph Tyler Flewelling (1871 – 1960). By that time, the focus of personalist writers had already shifted. Lotze and Bowne had focused on the question: what is the essence of a human being in a world seemingly functioning according to mechanistic laws? Flewelling focused much more on social issues:

> "To Personalism, personality is the supreme value. Society then should be so organized as to present to every person the best possible opportunity for self-development, physically, mentally and spiritually since the person is the supreme essence of democracy and hostile to totalitarianisms of every sort" (Flewelling, 1943).

Finally, some European names need to be mentioned. In Germany, a nun of Jewish descent, Edith Stein (1891-1943), focused on the notion of "empathy" (Einfühling), - experiencing how other people feel. Her thinking reflected a consideration, which in the mean time is widely held in personalist thinking – namely that being a person also means being with other persons. Edith Stein died in a nazi concentration camp.

In France, around the turn of the centuries, Charles Renouvier published *"Le Personnalisme"* (1903). Charles Renouvier struggled with the concept of determination in

35

history, as reflected in the thinking of his nineteenth century contemporaries Hegel and Marx. For him, determination went against his belief in human freedom. Renouvier also was a prolific political writer. Somehow, the French personalist tradition seems to have been close to politics. The European Christian-democratic tradition, for instance, was much influenced by the writings of two French personalists, Jacques Maritain and Emmanuel Mounier.

2.2 Nikolai Berdyaev (1874-1948): the Russian influence on French personalism

However, before getting to grips with the latter authors, we shall make a detour to Russia to familiarize with the thinking of Nikolai Berdyaev (1874-1948). Berdyaev was born in Kiev, a child of an aristocratic family, but turned to Marxism during his years as a student. For his role in political agitation, he was expelled by the Tsar regime to the north of Russia. After the October Revolution, the new Marxist government appointed him to a chair of philosophy at the University of Moscow, but he soon fell into disgrace for his independent political opinions. He was twice imprisoned and in 1922 was expelled from the country. While in exile, he lectured at the Sorbonne (Paris).

In an essay –Personalism and Marxism- published in 1935, Berdyaev compared his ideas on personalism with Marxism, the prevailing ideology in his native country. Before embarking upon the political discussion, however, he presented his views about the concept of the person.

> "It is not appropriate to confuse the concept of person with the concept of individual (...). The individual is a naturalistic category, biological and sociological, and it

36

appertains to the natural world. (...) Person signifies something altogether different. Person is a spiritual and religious category. Person speaks not only about man belonging to the natural and social order, but also to a different dimension of being, to the spiritual world. Person is a form of being, higher than anything natural or social." (Berdyaev, 1935)

This notion of the person, also resulted in pronounced views on the relation between person and society.

"Person is not determined by society, but it is social, it can realise the fullness of its life only in community with other persons. The social projection of personalism presupposes a radical, a revolutionary transvaluation of social values, i.e. the transfer of the centre of gravity from the values of society, the state, the nation, the collective, the social group, to the valuation of person, of every person." (Berdyaev, 1935).

His view on the uniqueness of every person, results in a rejection of sociological attempts to view persons in a one-dimensional way. This also leads him to a rejection of Marxism.

"Hostile to the principle of person is every single-planed world-outlook, for which the nature of man is comprised solely by its belonging to the social plane of being, i.e. man possesses no dimension of depth" (Berdyaev, 1935).

"Marxism is anti-personalist in that it posits the end-purpose not in man who is called to eternal life, but rather in society. The fundamental error basic to Communist Marxism is with this, that it believes in the possibility of coercive accomplishment not only of justice, but also of the brotherhood of people, in the possibility of coercive organisation not only of society, but also of community, of the communion of people.(...)" (Berdyaev, 1935)

In Berdyaev's thinking we see how the notion of the uniqueness of the human person is translated from an abstract philosophical premise into considerations of a political nature.

2.3 Jacques Maritain (1882-1973) and Emmanuel Mounier (1905-50): the personalist roots of European Christian-democracy

Similar political considerations were present in the writings of two French personalists, Jacques Maritain (1882-1973) and Emmanuel Mounier (1905-1950). Their ideas had a considerable influence on European Christian-democracy.

Jacques Maritain, Emmanuel Mounier and Nikolai Berdyaev all stayed in Paris at some time in the nineteen twenties and mutually influenced one another. They shared common concerns and common answers.

Maritain saw himself as working in continuity with the thinking of Thomas Aquinas, and at the time of his death, he was probably the best-known Catholic philosopher in the world. Maritain's most enduring legacy is undoubtedly his moral and political philosophy, and the influence of his work on human rights can be seen, amongst others, in the United Nations Declaration of 1948.

Following Aquinas, Maritain cherished the notion of natural law, - a legal and moral order governing all human beings. He believed that this natural law was 'written into' human nature by God. However, certain basic natural rights can be recognised by all, without there having to be agreement on their divine foundation. As an illustration of this, he pointed to the general agreement on those rights in the 1948 United Nations Declaration of Human Rights

Human beings are 'individuals' who are related to a common, social order of which they are parts. But they are also persons. The person is a 'whole' and must be treated as an end (Les droits de l'homme, p. 84). One is an individual in virtue of being a material being; one is a person in so far as one is capable of intellectual activity and freedom. Because of their individuality, human beings have obligations to the social order; because of their personality they cannot be subordinated to that order. Maritain's emphasis on the value of the human person has been described as a form of personalism, which he saw as a middle way between individualism and socialism.

Personalism, according to Maritain, requires interpersonal relations. Maritain stood for what he described as 'integral Christian Humanism' -- 'integral', because it considers the human Being as a unified whole with both material and spiritual dimensions and because it sees human beings in society as participants in a common good.

At the same time, he described his humanism as Christian, being rooted in the recognition of the human person as a spiritual and material being, with a relation to God. Man's natural rights, Maritain believed, ultimately stemmed from God's will and man's relation to God. Social and political institutions must reflect the high-exalted position of Man. He held that the authority to rule derives from the people -- for people have a natural right to govern themselves. Through this reasoning, he deducted his belief in American-styled democracy from

39

his Christian conviction. However, he did not favour capitalism and saw no link between capitalism and Christian conviction. The state policy should focus not so much on creating individual property but on providing the conditions for the realisation of the human person and on the common good. He extended his democratic beliefs beyond the classical liberal rights (such as parliamentary democracy), and also included for instance the rights of workers and the rights of people to participate in society through so-called civic fraternities. Given his Catholic background, he discussed primarily the role that could be played by Christian-inspired organisations in upholding moral and spiritual values that are needed to provide social cohesion. However, he recognized the differences of religious conscience and favoured a pluralistic state, which also valued the views of dissenting minorities.

Related views were held by Maritain's contemporary Emmanual Mounier, who was one of the founders of the influential French personalist magazine "l'Esprit". The following quotes reflect the thinking of Mounier.[7]

> "Personalism requires an affirmation of value, the affirmation of the absolute value of the human person. (...)"
> "A personalist society is one whose structure and spirit are directed towards the development as persons of all the individuals constituting it. They have as their ultimate end to enable every individual to live as a person, that is, to exercise a maximum of initiative, responsibility and spiritual life."

Although Mounier distanced himself both from fascism

---

[7]The quotes are selected from: Roots of the catholic worker movement. Emmanuel Mounier and Personalism.

and communism after the second world war, in the interwar period he was lured by the anti-individualism of both fascism and communism. Mounier's thinking after the second world war laid the foundation of the continental European Christian-democratic worker movement.

2.4 Shakçânyya

A little known brand of personalism is associated with the Moroccan author and philosopher Mohamed Aziz Lahbabi (1922-1993). With Lahbabi, we return to the African continent. Lahbabi studied philosophy at the Sorbonne in Paris, France. Throughout his life, he lectured at various universities, particularly at the Mohammed V University in Rabat (Morocco). In 1987 he was nominated as a candidate for the Nobel Prize of Literature. A particular focus of his work is the synthesis of Arab-Islamic and Western-humanistic ideas.

Although he has published a multitude of books and articles, his personalist views are best reflected in his 1964 book: *Le personnalisme musulman* (Muslim personalism).

Lahbabi introduces the word *"Shakçânyya"* as an Arab translation of "personalism". *Shakçânyya* is derived from the Arab "Shakç", meaning person. According to Lahbabi, Islam values the person in many respects. First of all, the human being is a sacred being. Animals too are part of the divine creation, but they lack the sacred qualities human beings are endowed with.

"He is a being who feels, lives and knows from his inner self that he lives and feels. He is capable of self-reflection, of distinguishing the different degrees of reality, of distinguishing ideas and sentiments that are right from those that are wrong, while animals live and

41

feel without ever examining their sentiments and ideas." (Lahbabi, 1964: 18).

Secondly, Islam, by calling people to testify of God, incites them to a personal quest for truth, devoid of clergical formalism. Through this open invitation, it values the human person as a free and thinking being. *"The YES of those who testify can only gain validity if there is also a possibility to say NO."* (Lahbabi, 1964: 68-70).

> "Personalism starts where the person refuses the blind submission to anyone or anywhat and recognizes the supreme value of reason and spirit. (...) 'There is no constraint in religion (II, 257)'. And hence no clergy, no intermediary between men and God. Every person is a creature created in a divine masterpiece, yet a unique creature. The human universe presents itself as book of infinite size, where the pages complement one another yet remain different: autonomous and interdependent." (Lahbabi, 1964: 7).

Thirdly, according to Lahbabi, Islam also recognizes the person in relation to others.

> "The person is an autonomous reality, yet in an interdepence – a communautarian I. To say I or me, also implies saying others. It means introducing an irreducible relationship. The I is autonomy in the interdependence of the "us." (Lahbabi, 1964: 23).

In pre-islamic times, he claims, people were not granted a proper personality. They were totally absorbed into the common identity of their tribe.

"To the contrary, in Islam, every human being is a person, independent of his ethnicity, his mother tongue, his skin colour... The 'adjami' (stranger) is a fellow-man of the Arab." (Lahbabi, 1964: 8).

Lahbabi's personalism also contains views about society and political life. In this respect, he quotes Abu-Bakr, the successor of the prophet Muhammed, and subsequently comments:

"In this way, Abu-Bakr formulates the principles of the Muslim ethical politics;
- equality before the Shari'a of the Caliph and the members of the Muslim community; conditional obedience of the latter to the former (one is not obliged to obey one's leaders if they do not adhere to the truth and to the will of God);
- to defend the weak against the abuse of power and to defend everyone against inequity.
- Also, there need be a democratic control on matters of public policy. Without this democratic control, the borderline between justice and injustice, between truth and lie, risks to disappear. (...) The Shari'a is an obstacle against those who can harm personal dignity by confounding morality and the fantasies and pleasures of power;" (Lahbabi, 1964: 55-57).

"The human being reasons. He derives his autonomy from his reasoning. Initiative, autonomy, reason, all constitute the human person and allow him to transcend the determinisms of nature, the social disorder and the tyranny of individuals and groups. Let us take the example of the State. This is constituted by human beings, but it may happen that it dehumanizes. The State depersonalizes people from the moment that it destroys the autonomy of the individuals."

The state is no substitute for personal ethical responsibility. Depersonalization starts when the State replaces all personal responsibility and starts to think and legislate on behalf of individuals (Lahbabi; 1964: 55).

> "The essence of personalism is the dignity of the human being and its fellowman. The dignity consists herein that we all become conscious of being worthwhile, that we have to embark on an adventure in our own universe, the adventure of a 'liberation' in the respect for the other. This freedoms imply our responsibility: solidarity and equality with all other persons. For the authentic Islam is, and could not be something else, than personalist." (Lahbabi, 1964: 104).

Lahbabi's *Shakçânyya* is not uniquely focused on abstract philosophical and religious matters, but also requires an engagement in the 'material' world.

> "Islam today should confront the industrial civilisation with a realistic mind, with new insights, engaged in the earthly problems. To the extent that they can reconcile 'heaven' and earth, religious beliefs and daily secular practice, Muslim renewers will be followed." (Lahbabi, 1964: 118).

In this respect, he also argues for the equality of men and women and for the recognition of the full rights of (religious) minorities.

2.5 Personalism: further developments

Some further developments of personalism need to be mentioned. First of all, a Central European branch of personalist thinking has sprung into the limelight. In

44

Poland, the personalist tradition is closely associated with the Catholic tradition of the country. The major personalist writer used to be Karl Woytila, who later became Pope John Paul II. His catholic orthodoxy on issues such as homosexuality and birth control has received much media attention and drawn an equivalent amount of controversy. This has obscured much of his personalist writings, which date back to a number of publications of the early sixties and to his lectures as professor in philosophy at the Catholic University of Lublin (Poland).

In his philosophical writings, Woytila pays considerable attention to the centrality of the human person. For Woytila, the centrality of the human person ultimately rests on a religious foundation.

> "If we celebrate with such solemnity the birth of Jesus, it is to bear witness that every human being is somebody unique and unrepeatable. (...) For God and before God, the human being is always unique... somebody thought of and chosen from eternity, someone called and identified by his own name."

Just like Mounier, Woytila points at the relational character of the human person. Once again, there is a religious connotation. As a being created in God's image, each human being is called to achieve the perfection of his own personhood by entering into genuine community with others. The potential to participate is essential to the self.

Also related to personalism are the writings of former Czechoslovakian dissident and Czech president Vaclav Havel. Across all cultures, Havel believes, there is a shared experience, a shared acknowledgement that there is something transcendental about being human. He

45

avoids the word God and instead refers to the universal experience of the human race:

> "there exist deep and fundamental experiences shared by the entire human race. Traces of such experiences can be found in all cultures, regardless of how distant or how different they are from one another". (Havel, 1995).

Human dignity is rooted in this transcendental awareness. From this reflection, he moves on to a variety of issues such as spirituality, personal responsibility and ethics. People should rediscover the common wisdom of the mythologies and religions of all cultures.

> "The relativization of all moral norms, the crisis of authority, reduction of life to the pursuit of immediate material gain without regard for its general consequences [originates] in that which modern man has lost: his transcendental anchor, and long with it the only genuine source of his responsibility and self-respect." (Havel: 1995)

The road to a global civilisation passes along notions such as human responsibility, the human power to reflect, wisdom, good taste, courage, compassion, and faith in the importance of particular measures. The reference to the importance of particular measures is a rebuff of mechanistic worldviews according to which history moves on in a predetermined way, making personal efforts redundant.[8]

While having been jailed because of his opposition to the Czechoslovakian communist regime, he also warns

---

[8]Havel criticized Marxism, in particular because of its claim that history is moved by a finite number of laws, driven by the ownership of the means of production and the class relations.

against too materialistic and utilitarian a culture.

> "Without a global revolution in the sphere of human consciousness, nothing will change for the better in the sphere of our being as humans, and the catastrophe toward which this world is headed – be it ecological, social, demographic, or a general breakdown of civilization -- will be unavoidable." (Havel: 1995).

In Western Europe, personalism is becoming increasingly detached from religious convictions. The human person is considered to be an end in itself, not necessarily because of his relation to God, but because of his inherent dignity. Not only does this evolution reflect the humanist tradition of this part of the continent, but even more the ongoing secularization of society. Church attendance is dropping. So are the religious certainties once cherished.

A last strand of thinking that needs to be mentioned is communautarianism. While communautarianism does not describe itself as personalist, there is a remarkable similarity in the way it looks at the role of the community. One of the principal authors is Amitai Etzioni, Professor and Director of the Center for Communautarian Policy Studies at the George Washington University.

> "The good society is one that balances three often partially incompatible elements: the state, the market and the community." (Etzioni, 2001: 6).

> "Communities provide bonds of affection that turn groups of people into social entities resembling extended families. Second, they transmit a shared moral culture form generation to generation, as well as reformulating this moral framework day by day." (Etzioni, 2001: 8).

47

"Seeking much greater reliance on communities is not an attempt to replace the welfare state. On the contrary, by reducing the burden on the welfare state, communities help sustain it." (Etzioni, 2001: 10).

2.6 Applied personalism: Christian-democracy as a political movement in Europe

European Christian democracy is a political movement, which sprung up after the Second World War.

Christian-democracy tries to translate personalist thinking into political practice. It is a secular movement, in that it wants to be independent of any particular confession. In practice, the degree of secularisation within the Christian-democratic parties has evolved with the secularisation of the society of which it was part.

The fundamental principle of Christian-democracy is the dignity of the human person. Christian-democracy recognizes that people are engaged in a diversity of social relations. First and foremost, we are part of a family. Through our children, we are part of the school community. At work, we meet our colleagues. Those of us who are practising believers, are part of a church community. We may be part of a hobby club. We may feel affinity to those whom we consider to be our cultural peers. We are citizens of our country. And so and so forth.

The reader will remember that one of the objections raised at Ubuntu, was the fear that the community would exert too stifling an influence on the individual. By recognizing the diversity of the communal circles, Christian-democratic theory circumvents this problem.

In political terms, this is done by invoking the principles of *subsidiarity* and *sphere sovereignty*.

Subsidiarity means that political competencies should

48

be transferred to the lowest level of government, unless there are good reasons to assume that a higher level of government is better placed to carry out a particular task. The subsidiarity principle originated in an epoch where totalitarian governments, Stalinist or fascist, were on the rise. As such, it was to safeguard society against the totalitarian state. In the mean time, it has evolved beyond this context and achieved a broad consensus as a principle, which favours the level of government that is closest to the people[9].

The notion of *"sphere sovereignty"* implies that the state, society, family, school and church comprise different spheres of responsibility and autonomy and are inviolable by one another. The state should not transgress into the autonomy of the other spheres – for, especially in politics, power must be limited in order to prevent abuse.

Originally, the principles of subsidiarity and sphere sovereignty were introduced as an antidote to the encroachment of state power. However, they were gradually elaborated into principles that encourage participation within the fabric of politics and society.

This is done by recognizing and supporting so-called mid-level organisations that function as intermediary between the individuals and the state. Among the classic examples are trade unions and employers' organisations. Yet at smaller local levels, one could also refer to parents' committees at school, self-help organisations, local community bodies..

These mid-level organisations do not only provide a means by which people can participate at various levels in

---

[9] The subsidiarity principles are enshrined, for instance, in the treaties of the European Union. Here, it means that the European Union assigns itself only a complementary role to the one of the member-states (or their underlying regional governments).

community life. Sometimes, they fulfil social responsibilities that would otherwise have been monopolized by
the state.

> "The tendency to view the state and the market as
> opposites (...) conceals the fact that some of the best and
> most important work of a society that aspires to be good
> is conducted either by the third sector or by hybrids.
> These are various amalgams in which elements of two
> or even three sectors are combined. Examples include:
> ೞReligious institutions and voluntary associations that
> provide social services, but are financed in part by the
> government;"
> (Etzioni, 2001: 28-29)

Christian-democracy stands for a slightly regulated
market economy with a comprehensive system of social
security and consultation. In post-war Germany, for
instance, the Christian-democratic government dismant-
led the government-controlled command economy
established by the Nazis. They strengthened the market
system by legislation to prevent the abuse of monopolistic
power. At the same time however, they established a
social security system and a system of consultation
between employer's organisations, trade unions and
government (the so-called Rhineland model).

Christian-democrats prefer the market economy, not
only because of its efficiency, but also because it
encourages human qualities like initiative and creativity.
The free market system is considered to be an alternative
against too much state power – and the risks of abuse
associated with it. Here, one recognizes the particular
time frame in which Christian-democracy originated: the
aftermath of the second world war, with the memories of
nazism still vivid and Stalin in power in the Soviet Union.

However, the dignity of the human person implies that he should neither be a victim of state power, nor of anonymous market mechanisms. Hence, policies to curtail the risks inherent to the market economy and to protect the weak. Finally, the consultation model stems from its endeavour to involve mid-level organisations.

Although for obvious reasons, the economy is considered to be of prime importance, the personalist outlook implies that the economy should not be *all pervasive*. This is reflected, for instance, in legislation to protect some spheres of life against dominance of the market forces. The examples are diverse and may vary from country to country. They may include -for instance- legislation to shield off some spheres of life from commercial advertising (without, however, an overall ban on advertising); an obligatory closing day for shops – so as to allow shop-owners a day of rest; subsidies for the press...

From the environmental point of view, Christian-democracy stands for "stewardship". Although human persons are considered to be superior to nature, they do not own the earth, nor nature. Solidarity is not limited to the present generation, but to the contrary, Earth should be safeguarded for next generations.

A final recurrent theme in Christian-democracy, is inter-state cooperation. Christian-democrats have consistently encouraged the formation of the European Union.

2.7 Critics

Personalism as a philosophical movement is not well known – partly because there is no one distinct personalist school.

A major point of controversy has been the relationship of personalism and religion. As we have seen, many personalist authors deduce the dignity of the human person from their belief in a personal God. For people who do not share this belief, this inevitably reduces the credibility of personalism. In this respect, we pointed at the fact that in Western Europe, which is becoming an increasingly secular society, personalism is becoming increasingly secular as well, maintaining its essential assumptions about the dignity of the human person, yet without recourse to God.

Another point of controversy relates to the respective roles of the individual and the community. Where exactly does the freedom of the individual end and do the rights of the community start? One recognizes here a similarity with an objection raised against Ubuntu. In reality, there have often been subtle differences among the personalist authors with regard to this question.

2.8 Summary

The philosophical roots of personalism go back to the nineteenth century, when it sought to affirm the centrality of the human person in an age marked by scientific discoveries and new insights.

In the first half of the twentieth century, personalism gradually took up political issues. It became concerned with the rise of totalitarian ideologies – national socialism and Stalinism, while at the same time rejecting the abuses inherent to unbridled capitalism. The dignity of the human person, the importance of interpersonal relations and the complementarity of the individual and the community became central themes. In Europe, personalism evolved into a political movement, known as

Christian-democracy.

A little known brand of personalism has been promoted by the Moroccan author, Mohamed Aziz Lahbabi. *Shakçanyya*, or Muslim personalism as he calls it, states that the dignity and the autonomy of the human person are explicitly recognized in Islam's invitation to a quest for truth, devoid of clergical formalism. Just like Ubuntu and Christian-democracy personalism, *Shakçanyya* pays much attention to interpersonal relations and the complementarity of the individual and the community.

CHAPTER 3

COMMON QUESTIONS, COMMON ANSWERS

In the preceding chapters, we paid attention to three distinct brands of thinking: African Ubuntu, Lahbabi's *Shakçânyya* and personalism. Although being rooted in three different civilisations, they display some remarkable similarities. Central to all three is the dignity of the human person and the complementarity of the individual and the community.

Can these common concerns, arisen in different settings, contribute to the dialogue of civilisations?

Please allow me now a personal touch. I believe that, across centuries and across civilisations, three fundamental fields of tension have stimulated political and philosophical thinking.

These questions are:

❑ The tension between the individual and the community.
❑ The tension between traditionalism and modernism.
❑ the status of Man: elevated or subject to nature?

How are Ubuntu, personalism and *Shakçânyya* positioned within these fields of tension?

3.1 The individual and the community

Throughout the ages, the tension between the rights

of the individual and those of the community has been prominent in political thinking.

At the same time, the belief in the complementarity of person and community reflects the concern to reconcile the following considerations:

❖ that personal autonomy be not sacrificed to the collectivity;
❖ that personal autonomy goes hand in hand with interpersonal relations and interpersonal solidarity.

While there may be subtle differences, there is common ground between African Ubuntu, (Christian-democratic) personalism and *Shakçânyya*.

The proponents of Ubuntu try to match the requirements of the market economy with their social concern and their concern about interpersonal relations. We encountered a similar balancing act in personalist thinking. Mounier and Maritain pointed at the risk of human abuse in capitalism. At the same time, Karl Woytila, writing from a different background (the communist regime in Poland), cautions against the state power developing into a totalitarian system where personal creativity is stifled. The balancing act resulted in a preference for a market economy with social corrections, a consultation model and legislation to safeguard certain spheres of life from the dominance of both the market economy and the power of the state.

Next to the economy, there is another domain that deserves to be mentioned: participation through mid-level organizations.

We described the role, which Ubuntu assigns to community-based organizations. At the same time, we noted the concern of its critics: conformity and peer pressure should not overwhelm the individual. The two sides of the coin point at the need for a balancing act: encouraging community building through interactive participation and simultaneously ensuring personal autonomy.

A similar concern appears in Christian-democratic personalism and *Shakçanyya*. By recognizing different layers of community Christian-democratic personalism allows for heterogeneity within the community. *Shakçânyya* performs the same balancing act.

> "The person is an autonomous reality, yet in an interdepence – a communautarian I. To say I or me, also implies saying others. It means introducing an irreducible relationship. The I is autonomy in the interdependence of the "us." (Lahbabi, 1964: 23).

3.2 The tension between traditionalism and modernism

Are our perceptions and convictions moulded by our cultural background or do we believe in people's ability to reason and transcend their own cultural background?

A glance at history reveals the omnipresence of this tension. In Europe, the French Revolution (1789) and Napoleonic expansion overthrew the traditional vestiges of power and introduced a whole set of administrative innovations. However, the introduction of these new structures often provoked local insurgencies. Modernism clashed with tradition. From its own perspective, Marxism shared the same revolutionary zeal. In Mozambique, the ruling party Frelimo transformed itself after independence into a Marxist-Leninist party. Adhering to the laws of "scientific socialism", it considered the existing traditional authorities as feudal and retrograde. As the euphoria

57

waned, so did the belief in the ability to transform society according to the laws of scientific socialism.

Ubuntu, personalism and *Shakçânyya* have the *potential* to position tradition and modernism as complementary to one another – not as opposites. *Shakçânyya* argues in favour of an intellectual quest for truth, devoid of any formalism. This clearly is a modernistic stance. Yet at the same time, Lahbabi's states that this is an inherently Islamic right and duty. In other words: modernism is legitimized by referring to the tradition.

Ubuntu's community focus is derived from the African communal way of living. However, at the same time there is an endeavour to match this romantic enchantment with modern day requirements –such as corporate life. This synthesis not only enhances the legitimacy of today's requirements but also facilitates the transition from the past to the present.

Christian-democratic personalism for its part, has in many respects been an agent of change. One of the principal examples is its contribution to the formation of the European Union, thus transcending the animosity that had resulted in two World Wars in less than half a century. Yet at the same time, it points at the diverse ways in which the person is related to the wider community.

This probably is the common message of Ubuntu, Lahbabi's *Shakçânyya* and personalism. Progress and change should never be forsaken. It is wrong to freeze society into imagined cultural and historical identities. However, it is equally wrong to believe that change can be implanted from above – with disregard for the local heritage. Rather, a synthesis is needed.

3.3 The status of Man: elevated or subject to nature?

Today, few philosophers, scientists or politicians wittingly doubt the status of the human person. I believe that such a reduction is much more an unintended consequence of different influences.

First of all, there was the spectacular progress of science, which started in the sixteenth century. On the one hand, science offered the human person perspectives, which he could never have dreamt of before: the capacity to cure diseases, to create welfare, to satisfy his intellectual curiosity. On the other hand, it dethroned Man from his pedestal. Man has been reduced to a tiny piece of 'dust' in the endless vastness of the universe.

More subtly, some ecological influences of the nineteen sixties and seventies also dealt human self-confidence a blow. In 1972, the Norwegian academic Arne Naess contrasted "shallow" and "deep" ecologism. "Shallow ecologists" promote the protection of the environment and the protection of the natural resources, but ultimately, nature remains at the service of the human being. Naess argued that this human-centred perspective should disappear. In 1975, the Australian author Peter Singer popularized, in his book 'Animal Liberation', the term 'speciecism':

> "a prejudice or attitude of bias in favour of the interests
> of one's own species and against those of members of
> other species."

To the contrary, personalism exalts the human person. It tries to reconcile this with ecological concerns through the notion of "stewardship".

The term "stewardship", which is used to typify the personalist approach to ecology, implicitly reflects this human-centeredness[10]. Environmental care and the preservation of earth's natural resources, in short - sustainable development- is called for, to preserve earth *for future generations* – not for earth's own sake.

In this field of tension (the status of Man: elevated or subject to nature) Shakçânyya too clearly recognizes the human person as a superior being.

> "He is a being who feels, lives and knows from his inner self that he lives and feels. He is capable of self-reflection, of distinguishing the different degrees of reality, of distinguishing ideas and sentiments that are right from those that are wrong, while animals live and feel without ever examining their sentiments and ideas." (Lahbabi, 1964: 18).

Ubuntu cherishes the qualities that make human beings truly 'personal' – referring to the spiritual character of the human person. We also demonstrated that human qualities like love and care are pivotal, not only in Ubuntu, but also in the writings of earlier authors like Senghor and Nyerere. These qualities (spirituality, love and care) are presented as truly human and inherently African. Nevertheless, there are some subtle differences with personalism and *Shakçânyya*. By distancing themselves from 'Western' thinking, some authors arrive at positions which closely resemble the 'deep' ecologism of Arne Naess. As such, Man is not longer elevated above "nature", but instead nature and Man are integrated into a holistic whole. Referring to the African, Senghor writes:

> "But he feels, he thinks that he can develop his potential, his originality, only in and by society, in

---

[10]In this respect, Naess would undoubtedly typify it as shallow ecologism.

union with all other men – indeed, with all other beings
in the universe: God, animal, tree or pebble." (Senghor,
1964: 94).

Nevertheless, we should be careful not to deduce from the
above statements that Ubuntu holds a "reductionist" view
on the human being. Elsewhere in the same book out of
which the above lines came, Senghor explicitly writes:

> "For the proper characteristic of Man is to snatch
> himself from the earth, to rise above his roots and
> blossom in the sun, to escape in an act of freedom from
> his 'natural determinations'. It is by liberty that man
> conquers nature and reconstructs it on a universal scale,
> that man realized himself as a god; this is freedom."
> (Senghor, 1964: 12).

I think that is fair to say that African Ubuntu, personalism
and *Shakçânyya* share a concern about the dignity of the
human person. From a different perspective, they all
arrive at an exalted view on the human person.

All this seems to be abstract. Are there any
implications? Without attempting completeness, I'd like
to single out the following items.

Corporate culture

In our review of African communalism of the sixties
and today's Ubuntu's philosophy, we saw an initial
predisposition against the market economy, followed by a
gradual coming to terms with the requirements and
advantages of the market economy. This coincides with
efforts to infuse into corporate life elements of
interpersonal relationships, consultation and consensus
seeking. Underlying, there is a concern that interpersonal

relations are not to be reduced to a mere economic interchange and that economic imperatives be reconciled with interpersonal relationships.

This concern is also a cornerstone of personalism. In several countries of continental Europe, this has resulted in the so-called Rhineland model (as opposed to the more Anglosaxon model). In the Rhineland model, the free market is complemented by consultations between the social partners (employers and trade unions) and a role for the state.

I believe that two elements are essential. A first challenge is to safeguard certain spheres of life from the encroachment of the economic logic. To say this does not mean that we disregard the need of economic growth. To the contrary, there is still too much poverty, too much unemployment, too much scarcity in the world. Yet not every aspect of our life should be subject to commercialisation.

A second challenge is to recognize that the market economy needs ethics to be structurally incorporated into it. Consumer legislation is needed to protect the consumer, accounting standards to ensure the transparency of balance sheets, labour legislation to protect employees, anti-cartel legislation to prevent distortion of competition and so on and so forth.

However, at the same time, the market economy itself remains a safeguard against too much power of the state.

These elements (the need to safeguard certain spheres of life from the encroachment of the economic logic, the need for structurally incorporated ethical values in the economy and safeguards against too much power of the state) are prominent in the writings of both secular and religious writers whom we encountered in the previous chapters.

62

Take the communautarian writer Amitai Etzioni.

"(the market economy) can provide an enormous bounty of products and services, and help to serve the common good.(...) However, it must be watched over carefully. If excessively restricted, the market economy cannot perform well. At the same time, a good society assumes that if the market is not properly contained, it may dehumanize people and wreck havoc on local communities, families and social relations." (Etzioni, 2001

From a religious point of view, Karl Woytila, in his capacity as Pope John Paul II, referred to these issues in his Papal Encyclical Letter Centesimus Annus[11]:

"The economy in fact is only one aspect and one dimension of the whole of human activity. If economic life is absolutized, if the production and consumption of goods become the center of social life and society ' s only value, not subject to any other value, the reason is to be found not so much in the economic system itself as in the fact that the entire socio-cultural system, by ignoring the ethical and religious dimension, has been weakened, and ends by limiting itself to the reduction of goods and services alone (....)" (John Paul II, 1991).

"If by "capitalism" is meant an economic system which recognizes the fundamental and positive role of business, the market, private property and the resulting responsibility for the means of production, as well as free human creativity in the economic sector, then the answer is certainly in the affirmative, even though it would perhaps be more appropriate to speak of a "business economy," "market economy" or simply "free

---

[11]Published in 1991, on the Hundredth Anniversary of Rerum Novarum

economy." But if by "capitalism" is meant a system in which freedom in the economic sector is not circumscribed within a strong juridical framework which places it at the service of human freedom in its totality and sees it as a particular aspect of that freedom, the core of which is ethical and religious, then the reply is certainly negative" (John Paul II, 1991)."

Societal pluralism

In personalism, *Shakçânyya* and Ubuntu, the human person does not stand on his own, but becomes more human in relation with other people. In this way, the relation between the person and the community is not a coercive one, but an enabling one.

Many of the present-day tensions stem from the assumption that one particular sphere of society claims supremacy. For instance, religious fundamentalism – from whatever origin- attributes absolute truth to the prevailing religion. Cultural nationalism hails the (presumed) collective cultural identity to such an extent that it overwhelms the individual identity. Consumerism reduces the human person to the role of mere consumers and confuses market economy with market society.

If one assumes that the different spheres of society all have their proper role, one is less inclined to claim supremacy for one particular sphere. To continue with the example: the trouble is not religion, nor cultural heritage or consumption. The trouble is the claim of supremacy for one of these.

By pointing at the complementarity of human persons and community through a _multitude_ of relationships, personalism, *Shakçânyya* and Ubuntu could contribute to such a pluralism.

This has a double dimension. On the hand – to protect the human person against the encroachment of

64

any particular sphere. In this sense, political power should never be more than a constrained delegation. The ones elected to government are given this mandate during a limited time-span and within constitutional constraints. Similarly, while it implies that the state should not impose religion or any philosophy upon its citizens, it also implies that certain spheres of life should remain safeguarded for people to practice, search or belief (whatever may be the case).

On the other hand, it also has a positive dimension – enabling people to participate through a variety of means in wider society. A whole range of examples can be quoted: from family life to local community participation, the Ubuntu-view on consultation and consensus-seeking in corporate life; the Rhineland model...

Sustainable development and a human person - centred ecology

To what extent are human beings entitled to "exploit" nature? Earlier, we referred to the "deep ecologism" of Arne Naess and "Animal Liberation" of Peter Singer. Both authors reject, one way or another, the human-centred notions of economic and technological progress. By raising nature to the level of Man, they have implicitly dethroned Man from his pedestall.

Personalism, *Shakçânyya* and Ubuntu all cherish the human person. Yet at the same time, Ubuntu and African communalism, by distancing itself from "Western" materialistic thinking, reject the utter submission of nature for mere economic purposes. Is there a common ground?

We all need nature for enjoyment. Who does not feel relaxed after a good hike? However, nature is not a natural ally. Many deadly diseases are part of nature as well. Economic and scientific progress has reduced our

65

vulnerability towards nature.

Obviously, this should not blind us for some very acute ecological problems. Yet at the same we should be aware that underdevelopment too has a heavy ecological toll. Just think about erosion due to overgrazing or deforestation due to excessive wood gathering.

I do believe that there could be a common ground for personalism, *Shakçânyya* and Ubuntu, through the notion of stewardship. We do not own nature, but we can utilize it temporarily, we are 'stewards'. This means that we can exploit nature, yet in doing so, we should be careful not to spoil it for next generations. In other words: sustainable development.

This approach represents a human-centred ecology. The human person remains pivotal, be it not only the present generation, but also future generations.

Concluding remarks

We compared Ubuntu, Christian -democratic personalism and Shakçânyya - political philosophies that originated in different contexts, in different continents and different civilisations. Despite the different setting in which they originated, they invoke similar concerns and similar questions.

Moreover, we also discovered similarities in the answers they provided. I hope that the awareness of common questions and common answers may be helpful to erode the stereotyped views that are held of one another.

Bibliography

Biko, Steve (1987), I write what I like: a selection of his writings. (Penguin Books, London)

Beke, Wouter (2007), De mythe van het vrije ik. Pleidooi voor een menselijke vrijheid (Averbode)

Boon, Mike (1996), The African Way: the power of interactive leadership (Zebra Press, Sandton).

Etzioni, Amitai (2001), The Third Way to a Good Society. In: Sociale Wetenschappen, 44ste jaargang, nr.3

Havel, Vaclav (1995), Democracy's Forgotten Dimension, in: Journal of Democracy 6, no. 2 (April 1995).

Hlongwane, Nhlanhla, In the Battle-Front with Learnered Elder Dr. Ntate Koka.

Houtondji, Paulin (1983), African Philosophy: Myth and Reality. (Hutchinson University Library for Africa, London).

Kuada, John (ed) (2008) , Challenges of Enterprise-driven Economic Growth in Africa. The African Journal of Business and Economic Research, Vol. 3, No 1. 2008 (Adonis & Abbey, London)

Khoza, Reuel (2006), Let Africa Lead (Vezubuntu, Sunninghill)

Lahbabi, Mohamed Aziz (1964), Le personnalisme

Musulman. (Presses Universitaires de Paris, Paris).

Lascaris, Reg & Lipkin, Mike (1993), Revelling in the Wild: Business Lessons out of Africa (Human & Rousseau, Cape Town).

Lukhele, Andrew Khehla (1990), Stokvels in South Africa (Amagi Books, Johannesburg).

Maluleke, Tinyiko Sam: African intellectuals and the white academy in South Africa --- some implications for Christian theology in Africa

Mandela, Nelson (1978), The struggle is my life (IDAF, London)

Mbeki, Thabo (1998), Africa: the time has come. (Tafelberg Publishers, Cape Town).

Mbiti, John (1969), African Religions and philosophy (Praeger, New York).

Moita, L (1980), De Kongressen van het Frelimo, de PAIGC en de MPLA: een vergelijkende analyse (De Uitbyt).

Padmore, George (1960), Panafricanisme ou communisme (Présence Africaine).

Senghor, Léopold (1964), On African Socialism (Praeger, New York).

Setiloane, Gabriel (1988), Civil authority from the perspective of African theology, in: Journal of Black

Theology in South Africa, vol.2, No. 2, 11 nov, 1988. (p16-23), 11

Shutte, Augustine (1998), Philosophy for Africa (UCT Press, Cape Town).

Sono, Themba (1994), Dilemmas of African intellectuals in South Africa (UNISA, Pretoria).

Information available on the internet:

Berdyaev, N (1935), Personalism and Marxism. (http://www.krotov.info/engl/berdyaev/1935_400.html)

Capps, Walter (1997), Interpreting Vaclav Havel, in: Cross Currents, Fall 1997

Casa Juan Diego, Roots of the Catholic Worker Movement: Emmanuel Mounier and Personalism. (http://www.cjd.org/paper/roots/remman.html)

John, Paul II (1991), Centesimus Annus. (www.newadvent.org/docs/jp02ca.htm)

Kelder, Dirk (1998), Berdyaev's Philosophy (http://www.chebucto.ns.ca/Philosophy/Sui-Generis/Berdyaev/bp.htm)

Louw, Dirk (2002), Ubuntu and the challenges of Multiculturalism in post-apartheid South Africa. (http://www.phys.uu.nl/~unitwin/ubuntu.html)

Mbigi, Lovemore (2000), Managing Social Capital.

(http://www.findarticles.com/cf_0/m4467/1_54/59138077/print.jhtml)

Nyerere, Julius, Kambarage: Ujamaa: the basis of African Socialism.
(www.nathanielturner.com/ujamaanyerere.htm)

Sweet, William (1997), Jacques Maritain (Stanford Encyclopedia of Philosophy).
(http://plato.stanford.edu/entries/maritain)

Index

71

Notes

Notes

Notes